Living Out Transparent Faith

Words of Advice + Scriptural Direction on Living Boldly and Transparently for Jesus

Lauren Faith McRoberts

ISBN 978-1-64299-203-8 (paperback)
ISBN 978-1-64299-204-5 (digital)

Copyright © 2018 by Lauren Faith McRoberts

All rights reserved. No part of this publication may be reproduced, distributed, or transmitted in any form or by any means, including photocopying, recording, or other electronic or mechanical methods without the prior written permission of the publisher. For permission requests, solicit the publisher via the address below.

Christian Faith Publishing, Inc.
832 Park Avenue
Meadville, PA 16335
www.christianfaithpublishing.com

All scriptural references are from the NIV translation.
Page 18 image is taken by Andrea Wood.
Page 119 image is taken by Gracie Days.
All other images are courtesy of Lauren Faith Photography.

Printed in the United States of America

To my parents, for the truth they've constantly
spoken in me for the past sixteen years
Mama and Daddy,
I love y'all with my whole heart.

CONTENTS

Foreword for Lauren..7
Introduction...9
Chapter 1: My Story 11
Chapter 2: Transparency is Key............................29
Chapter 3: Walking in the Light (in Three Parts) 35
            Part 1: Where Did Everyone Go?................35
            Part 2: "I'll Never Be Enough" 40
            Part 3: "Tempted" 48
Chapter 4: House of Prayer...................................52
Chapter 5: Uphill Battle...58
Chapter 6: Joy and Happiness: What's the Difference?...65
Chapter 7: "Where Are You?"................................73
Chapter 8: In Love with Love (featuring a letter
            to my girls) 77
Chapter 9: True to You..84
Chapter 11: *Tetelestai* 89
Acknowledgments 93

FOREWORD FOR LAUREN

When Lauren reached out to me, I was so honored to say the least. Lauren spends her day-to-day encouraging men and women in their daily lives to live out their purpose and to walk in love. I had the incredible opportunity to read this book, and I am so proud of her. I also KNOW ya'll are going to love and soak in these words. The best way I could sum this book up for you is "encouragement explosion". That's what I felt as I read this, and that's what I know you will experience within the pages of this book. Not only is this major encouragement, this book is so practical to apply to daily life. From personal experience, writing a book is no walk in the park. On Lauren's behalf, I think she would want you to know how thankful she is that you picked this book up. Seriously. She believes in this message and I do too. I hope it blesses you (I know it will). Now get started reading the book! I'm not going to spoil anything, so if you read this for that reason, you're out of luck.

- Chelsea Crockett

INTRODUCTION

Hey, friend, Lauren here. So you obviously are about to start reading my book. Before you begin, there are a few things I wanted to share with you:

1. Open your heart.
2. Open your mind.
3. I don't cover *every* struggle you may face as a young Christian, but I do speak to some of the most prominent. However, be in the Word. Back my words up with scripture.
4. Lastly, what you're about to read is straight from experience and straight from my heart.

I pray as you begin to read this, you keep an open mind and heart and that the Lord works in you like He did me while writing this.

Okay, I think you're ready. I poured my heart out onto paper for you.

In Christ and with so much love,
Lauren Faith

CHAPTER 1

MY STORY

I'm going to tell you a story—one about a young girl who knew nothing different than to be at church anytime the doors were open. One about a girl with wide eyes and a childlike faith with dreams bigger than she believed she could ever achieve.

I don't really have what you would call a superdrastic, exciting testimony.

You see, I grew up in church. Well, I still am growing up in church; the same church, that is. Growing up somewhere for sixteen years is kind of unheard of. Nowadays, people do what I like to call "church hop" where if the pastor says one thing you don't like, disagree with, or take offense to, that's it. You leave and find a new church body. And it's a never-ending, vicious cycle. I'm honestly so blessed (I know; and, no, not #blessed) I am a teenager, but I'm not your typical sixteen-year-old. Anyways, for my parents to join a church family and stay committed to that family for so long is honestly such a huge blessing, and I know that I'm super fortunate to have experienced church in that sense. Now, I am super passionate about the church; no, not the building. I believe that a church is a body of believers—real human beings with souls—and in this case, ones that are the hands and feet of Jesus. Humans who uplift each other and get down into the ditch with you to help you, not just pull you out. I realize that this is far-fetched from what the "church" is really like in today's society; but I'd like to believe that in Heaven, where everything is perfect, all the church will do is serve and love one another.

Okay, now that that rabbit trail has gone down, I can get back to the story.

So I grew up in church and was there every Sunday morning and night whether it be for kid's choir or life group or just to be there in general. I grew up with my parents teaching me Sunday school all throughout elementary school. Now, my mama teaches me as a senior in high school, while my dad is in children's ministry teaching one of my three siblings' classes. Remember what I said about being in the same place for a long time and how it's unheard of? Well, as you might've figured out, I never really moved either growing up. I grew up in the Midlands and never knew anything different, although I'm an avid "road-tripper." So as I got older, you can find me in neighboring cities or even states exploring.

You see, from the outside, my life was "picture perfect"—my parents together, the oldest of four beautiful kids, never moved communities, had Jesus in my heart, honor-roll student, has many friends, loved to sing, and so on.

Sounds perfect, huh?

Some might say so. I really do, and I did have a great childhood. With my parents both coming from broken homes, I know what turmoil and baggage that can bring in families. Trust me, I do know. And as a family of six, we never really had many major issues within our family dynamic. Yes, there were many tense dinners, arguments, and fights; but as for real, big, earthshaking issues, we had none. We were solid.

So with that being said, as far as my personal walk with the Lord, I prayed to receive Christ one night with my mama and daddy, as well as our children's pastor in the parlor of our old church campus, after a lesson spoke to my heart as a young seven-year-old. That might spark some controversy right there—some might say that I could've never understood the meaning of salvation, or that I was a sinner whose Savior died for her. I can understand where you're coming from in thinking that, but I honestly believe with all of my heart that Jesus changed my life that night.

However, with that being said, it wasn't until sixth grade that I truly started realizing that this lifestyle—the Christian lifestyle—was one that required daily surrender and a purposeful intention to live for Jesus. When I entered into middle school, I started struggling majorly with my "friends." I guess you could say it was a typical teenage-girl drama, but to me at that time, walking those hallways was like walking through fire. I can remember one specific time period where a really hateful rumor was spread about me, and I'll never forget the day I begged my mom to let me stay home. If you asked my peers now, they probably wouldn't even remember this incident; but to me, my self-esteem was at an ultimate low. For me to miss school was a big deal.

Before seventh grade, I never had made a B on my report card or taken anything less than advanced and honors courses. Needless to say during middle school, my world was rocked to the core. Classes got harder and more intense, reputation started becoming important, I had a boy I was head over heels for, and everything was becoming way more serious than I had planned for and way too quickly. As far as extracurricular activities, I've never been an athletic person other than dance, I love to dance. Was I a competitive dancer with all three of her splits and beautiful pirouettes? Absolutely not. But give me some choreography and some fun music, and I was there with overflowing passion.

While dancing will always hold a dear place in my heart, singing and my passion for music was where my heart was. I was in choir from elementary school all the way up until I started homeschooling in high school. I was a part of several district honor choirs and region choir as well as various other fun groups along the way. In fact, one of my most fond memories of middle school was my participation in our praise team at church. When I was twelve, as soon as I moved up from kid's ministry into student ministry, I moved on from being in the kid's musicals to singing in the youth group's praise team. I actually still, to this day, sing in our youth's praise band which has turned from an acoustic guitar and a tambourine with occasional piano to a full drum set, three people on vocals, a bass, acoustic, and two electric guitars. Quite the upgrade, huh? I love it with all of my heart. And if you knew me, you'd know that while I love being up there leading my peers in worship, when the spotlight fades, instruments quieted, and the soundboard turned off, I am all about genuine worship. What do I mean by that? That will be discussed later.

Besides the point, worship through song and just singing in general was and still is a huge part of who I am.

*****

Moving past sixth grade, in seventh and eighth grades were really where I started realizing and living out my faith with complete boldness and with everything in me. I was on my middle school's FCA leadership team all throughout junior high and led my peers in prayer at lunch in the cafeteria, called them out on their cuss words, the whole nine yards. I was living my life completely sold out for Jesus, or so I thought, while getting ridiculed for it as any middle schooler would at some point.

The thing is, though, is your faith really the same when you're in the cafeteria at school versus when you're completely alone at home? Is your faith from the outside really what matters if on the inside? Or is it the complete opposite? I'll give you a hint: No, it's not. I could care less at what your Instagram bio is or what Bible verse is in it. If your mouth is complete filth or you're completely living for the world when no one's watching, I promise you: Jesus could care less about what mask we put on. If we aren't truly living and worshipping Him in every aspect of our life, there's a deeper issue. I'm sorry if that sounds harsh, but it's true, and this is just the beginning of the raw issues I'm going to discus throughout this book. If you aren't open to conviction in your own life or perhaps ready to learn with me, you can go ahead and close the book now and stop reading. My whole purpose for this book is to learn with you and speak truth into your life from a perspective of real experiences and words the Lord has laid on my heart.

Don't get me wrong. Please, please, please pray at your lunch table and hold your friends accountable. But when you do it, check your heart and your intentions first before you try to call someone else out on their issues.

In all reality, when 100 percent living for Jesus gets hard, it is when your faith is tested; and that "picture-perfect" lifestyle that I talked about gets turned upside down.

This happened for me in the eighth grade.

In all, eighth-grade year was tough, but it was a year of monumental growth. Physically, yes; but more so emotionally, mentally, and spiritually.

Before I get to the rest of the story, I want you to know that there isn't always a happy ending. I don't mean to rain on your parade, but for me, this year of my life was circumstance after circumstance of pain.

*****

This year of my life was hell. (Sorry for the drastic word, but I promised you I would be nothing but raw and real with you.)

The summer before I started my last year of middle school, I decided to join my soon-to-be high school's dance or color guard team. This team was a mixture of sideline dancers, which mostly consisted of the girls that had been dancing competitively their whole life—understandably so, of course. The other part of the team, the color guard, was split into another two parts: flags and rifles or sabers. If this sounds foreign to you, let me make it easier.

You know the half-time show during football games? Okay, so along with the band (Woohoo! go band.), there are the flag spinners, sabers—or as you might see it—sword spinners, and the ones that toss what looks like a gun—the rifles. Now in high school, at least where I'm from, being in color guard or band isn't exactly what you'd call the best thing for your reputation. If you were a sideline dancer, that's a whole other story. They got the sparkly outfits and their own side of the field along with some killer choreo- that I promise you I couldn't do even if I spent years trying. My legs don't bend that way, ha!

Anyways, back to the story. So I joined Gatorettes. This was just the beginning of the year that I like to call my "perfect storm." At the end of the summer, we had band camp, which is the three excruciatingly long weeks devoted to running laps; learning extremely hard drills; and for me, as a Gatorette, never ending squats. I could hardly sit down for weeks on end.

And, no, I'm not one-bit exaggerating. Ask anyone of the "Fierce 51." For what it's worth, to be so lame to our peers, we had a pretty cool name for our team.

So, band camp probably was the hardest three weeks of my life—physically, at least. Emotionally, I was drained as well. I didn't have what you would call the most encouraging coach. In fact, I can remember several vulgar things that were yelled to me across the field by said coach that certainly did nothing good for my already sensitive, middle-school-girl self-esteem.

To add to this, during the second week, my family was gone at the beach while I was staying with my grandma at home. Don't get me wrong; I love my GG. She's my best friend, but nothing compares to your mama's embrace when you've had a hard day or week, in my case. Turns out, actually that week, I ended up having my first full-blown anxiety attack.

Now at the time, I had no idea that's what it was, but I can precisely remember what was one of the scariest moments of my life.

I couldn't catch my breath.

My vision was blurred.

I could hardly stand up.

My legs felt like they were failing underneath me as I leaned up against my flag pole in the middle of the band field.

My heart was pounding out of my chest.

This wasn't your typical "let me catch my breath, inhale for four seconds, exhale for the same" type of anxiety attack. I honestly felt like I was going to die. Once I wasn't completely disoriented, I ran off the field and can vaguely remember the long walk to the band closet where my phone was. I called my grandma, whom I was staying with for the week, and told her what was going on.

One thing you should know about my grandma is that she has extensive knowledge and experience in the medical field. So as I told her my symptoms through my scattered breaths, she was frantic. She immediately came up to the school, and she actually was starting to take me to the emergency room. I'm assuming her thought process was of our family's extensive list of cardiac problems. Even just how when added up, my symptoms were pretty scary. I convinced her to just take me home where I called my mama and cried to her while telling her what I had just experienced.

She simply said, "Sweetie, I think what you just experienced was an anxiety attack."

Little did I know, that was the beginning of what I thought at the time was the end.

The next few weeks went by, and I did—in fact—push through the last couple weeks of band camp. Then my eighth-grade year started. I made it through the first few months with little to no problems as far as any more major anxiety issues.

Disclaimer: I've always had anxiety. I'm what you could call a definite worrier. I mostly just brushed it off to the only "normal" I knew. After all, a little bit of anxiety was normal. So eighth-grade year went by; and then in the spring, the "hell" that I was talking about started. To any of my then classmates or peers reading this, you might be surprised at what you're about to read.

*****

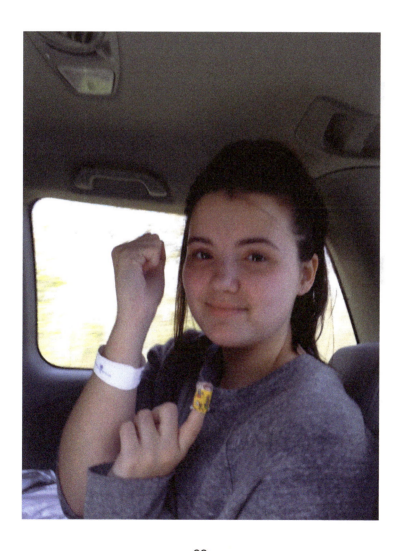

In the spring, I started missing school days and weeks at a time. While I've always struggled with chronic headaches and migraines, my pediatrician just kept on writing doctor's excuses so my mom wouldn't have truancy filed against her.

Then, I missed three whole weeks of school.

Yep, *three. Whole. Weeks.*

And, yes, my inner honor-roll student was absolutely freaking out. Trust me, I tried to push through the hard days. I'd show up to school, but then my first-period teacher would call my mom herself and tell her to come dismiss my weary looking self. At first, we thought it was a virus. I could hardly get out of bed whether it was just weakness, body aches, severe stomach pain, or dizziness. It was always something. I simply did not have the strength to lift myself up out of bed. When about a week and a half went by, we thought it was time to visit the doctor again. She said it could be mononucleosis or mono. Come to find out, when my blood results came back, she said the mono test came back negative; however, I was borderline anemic. Yes, along with my everyday pains, I wasn't eating either. My blood sugar was at an all-time low all the time.

Yet still, we thought it was a virus.

After weeks upon weeks of using my mom's support to walk around the house and not leaving my room, I finally went back to school.

*****

Fast forward a few summer months, I was entering my freshman year of high school. I brushed off what you would call your normal everyday jitters as you would and should get as a high school freshman.

Then the cycle started again. I was in and out of school for what seemed like every other day with "viral-like" symptoms.

In October, one specific night I remember so vividly, I was sitting on the couch while my GG was playing with my hair, and I was talking to my mom about the hard day or week I was having.

And I lost it. It was like months' worth of emotions just billowed out of me all at once.

It was in that moment that I stopped fighting it.

I was, and had been, struggling with depression and severe anxiety.

The next few days and weeks consisted of my mom making countless phone calls to psychiatrists and various specialists. I was then put on waiting list after waiting list. Fast forward to December, no head way in my mental health had been made, I started having severe pelvic and stomach pain. I was then diagnosed with PCOS, otherwise known as polycystic ovarian syndrome. I'm not going to go into detail about what this consists of, but it's any person's nightmare when you have cysts rupturing in your lower stomach constantly.

After still missing occasional days at school and having a really hard time socially and academically, at this point after being distanced and absent in my relationships with others along with a whole lot of other struggles that come with mental illness, my parents were determined to do whatever it takes to get me into see someone even if it meant dipping into finances we wouldn't don't have. We waited to be at the top of the waiting lists. Little did we know, if we had waited, we wouldn't have gotten a call from those various offices until *April*.

*****

So January comes, and after seeing my doctor and finally being taken seriously, I was put on medicine. At this point, along with my family, I made the decision to drop out of public school and start homeschooling. When we finally got my medicines right and I was well on my way to being back to my normal self, my freshman year was coming to a close.

I will talk more about my journey with anxiety and depression later, but for now, I'm trying to keep it basic.

Needless to say, homeschooling was one of the best decisions I've made for myself ever. I ended up skipping sophomore year and thriving academically, which brings me to now. I'm currently a sixteen-year-old senior in high school. I take care of two beautiful kids, which has been one of the many perks that come from homeschooling—freedom with my time. Speaking of my time, I either spend it writing (blogging); singing at church; taking road trips with my closest friends, which happen to be my mom and grandmothers; or spending time at home with my dog, Brunson, and my three little siblings.

Now, enough about me. I totally understand if that was entirely too agonizing to read, but I just wanted to put everything out in the open before I dig deeper into my personal experiences and how they've shaped me. As for the next chapter, I'm so excited to learn and grow with you and embark on a journey of talking openly about real struggles we face as Christ's followers, which brings me to this: If you currently aren't following Jesus, I encourage you to keep on reading anyways; and maybe, just maybe, you'll learn a little something as well.

So, my friend, let's get started!

LAUREN FAITH McROBERTS

CHAPTER 2

TRANSPARENCY IS KEY

When I was a freshman in high school and I started homeschooling, I decided to start a blog. Part of this decision was just to simply have a way for my friends to keep up with me while I wasn't seeing them every day. But the other part, perhaps the biggest part of me wanting to do this, was that writing had always been extremely therapeutic for me. When I started blogging, I knew I wanted it to be faith-based and for me to be completely real, raw, and transparent with my readers which, at the time, starting out was probably with just my parents and their Facebook friends. (shout-out to my "day 1" supporters, ha!)

So this blog was called *Living Out Transparent Faith*. It was made on the most basic DIY website software from WordPress. Now I have nothing against anyone who uses this; in fact, if you're just starting out blogging or having a website in general, I highly recommend starting out basic. I am, for sure, no graphic designer. Okay, back to the point. My point is it was nothing fancy, and I had no idea what my purpose was for it other than to make myself feel better by putting words down on paper and maybe share a little truth along the way.

In fact, a quote from my first blog post, written in December 2015, is this:

> As Christians, or just normal people, we put on what I like to call, our "Sunday morning smiles" and pretend like everything is okay when in fact, we're struggling. This blog will focus on what it means to have transparent faith when life hands you opaque situations.

This quote, apparently something that was on my heart two years ago, is still something that lies heavy on my heart as I'm writing this for you today. You might ask, "What exactly is 'transparent faith'?" Or "Why is transparency so important?" Hence, that is the name of the chapter: "Transparency is Key."

Well, lucky for you, I'm going to answer those two questions and many more you might have thoroughly throughout the next few pages.

*****

To me, transparent faith is when someone does not hide their faith. They do not hide their struggles nor do they hide their triumphs.

As you probably learned in elementary-school science, transparent means clear. Likewise, the opposite of transparent is opaque 'when you can't see through something.'

Transparent faith is letting others see Jesus through *everything* you do—not just your social media or while around certain people—and using your trials *and* triumphs for His glory. If your Instagram bio has a Bible verse in it, but at school or work, you've got a dirty mouth or non-pure relationship, are you living transparently? Is your faith transparent?

Living out your faith transparently isn't the only important thing about transparency. It is also extremely important to be transparent with *yourself* and others. You might be thinking, how in the world can I not be transparent with myself? Let me say this: When I was struggling immensely with my personal health in the eighth grade, I was not being transparent with myself. I needed to wake up and realize that there was a deeper issue. Another example was when I was in middle school and I thought I had everything together, and I took it upon myself to call my friends out on their problems before checking myself first. I was not being transparent with myself then either.

If you're struggling with something, the biggest step in improving it is realizing that you have that problem first and being 100 percent transparent with yourself.

It is also extremely important to be transparent with others as well. Remember what I said about "Sunday morning smiles"? What I mean is that often times when we come into other people's presence or see a certain someone, we often put on this "mask," pretending everything is okay when really it's not.

When you begin to be transparent with others, so much bondage that you might not even know is there is broken. When I started struggling with depression, my first instinct was to crawl into an "emotional hole" and hide my struggles from everyone. Now when I decided to break free from that and open up about what I was dealing with, so much weight was lifted up off of my shoulders. I like to say that "chains were broken" because that's what it felt like. It felt like this bondage and chains that had been entangling me (kind of like it says in Hebrews 12) fell off, and I could finally live in full freedom.

I can't begin to tell you how much being transparent has impacted and bettered my life.

For me, the way I started being transparent was to open up in writing. So like I mentioned at the beginning of this chapter, I started a blog. That might sound extreme to you—opening up to the internet (theoretically the whole world) about my deepest rooted issues; but for me, it was my own form of therapy. Not only did this benefit me personally, but people started to open up to themselves and others. Jesus used me as a vessel for other transparency to start taking place. I know this because I can vividly remember as soon as I published the blog post about my struggle with clinical depression and anxiety, a girl I had been going to school with for years contacted me about how she had been struggling with the same things.

I was in awe, not of myself, but of Jesus and what He had just done.

Because I felt being led and decided to be transparent about my hurt and what was going on in my life, another person's life was changed. In fact, she was the first of many people who opened up to me about how they were struggling with the same things I was.

And you know what the crazy thing is? I thought I was alone. And, yes, transparency can be extremely difficult; but like most things, in the end, it's totally worth it.

You see, because I felt Jesus leading me to be transparent, it opened up a wave of others who did the same. And because of that, all of these people discovered that they weren't alone.

*****

Transparency is so, so, so important in your faith, in your relationships, and in your life. In fact, I believe it's the key.

So be transparent regardless if life seems to be opaque. I promise you, the freedom you will feel will be exhilarating. You'll never regret it.

Because of my transparency, Jesus turned my MESS into a MESSAGE and my TRAGEDY into a TRIUMPH.

And, friends, I came to find out and am here to tell you now that that was just the beginning.

CHAPTER 3

WALKING IN THE LIGHT (IN THREE PARTS)

Part 1: Where Did Everyone Go?

A wise woman who just so happens to be a former teacher-turned best friend of mine once said this: "Sometimes it's lonely walking in the light."

Friends, let me be honest with you for a second. I've never related with something any more than I did in that moment when I heard those words come out of her mouth.

Walking with Jesus is hard, period. Some people have this false reality that when you give your heart to Jesus, it's all sunshine and rainbows for the rest of your life into eternity. Remember how I said a little earlier that part of what I wanted people to get from my writing was a little bit of truth? Well, I'm going to let you in on a piece of truth right now. You ready?

It. Is. Not. Easy. Walking. With. Jesus. Never has, never will be.

Now don't get me wrong. When you give your heart and soul to Jesus, you obtain and overflow with this unexplainable joy that you'll never experience otherwise. However, going against the flow—period—is hard. It always will be. Therefore, sometimes you're going to feel alone.

A big stepping stone, learning experience, epiphany—whatever you may call it—took place my freshman year of high school. This took place during some of the darkest moments of my life, so far, but I realized that it's *a lot*. I mean, it is a lot easier living for the world than it is to live for Jesus; now, granted I was in my first year of high school and surrounded by lost teenagers that had no idea what their purpose was, but still.

I was living for Jesus. And I was lonely.

When I say that word "lonely," you probably picture me in a corner, completely isolated from everyone around me—no friends and such. That's just the thing. I was surrounded by so many people, had so many "friends," was well liked, the works; but I've come to find out that when you're lonely, the easiest thing to do or the easiest way to hide was to be in a crowd.

I know. That's deep, huh?

I felt so alone, and sometimes I still do.

But let me tell you about this guy I know.

His name is Jesus, and He will take all of your feelings of loneliness away just at the mention of His name. That may sound super cliché to you, but it's so true.

I'm tellin' ya, if I didn't know Jesus during these periods in my life when I felt lonely, I don't know what I would do. You might be thinking, "Lauren, why are you telling me this? Are you throwing a pity party?"

No, I'm definitely not. I'm here to tell you that in fact, you aren't alone. Another cliché, I know. But for real.

I can't remember how many times I sat "alone" in a crowd of people or how many days or weeks I went without having someone to talk to or relate with. And this isn't just for you teenagers; it's for you adults too. I know school, the work place—wherever you may be—can be lonely sometimes. In today's society, living sold out for Jesus or as I like to say "walking in the light" is not only hard, but it's also extremely hard to find someone to share in your faith and share in your struggles. And, friends, I can't tell you how important it is to find someone, a peer, that you can confide in.

If you don't get anything else I say in this chapter, get this: You can't do life alone. In fact, if you have Jesus, you won't be alone. Don't take for granted the people you have in your life that can share in your struggles, rejoice with you in your triumphs, and talk about Jesus with you. These people are precious, and they're crucial. And if you're going through a period of time like me where you feel like you don't have any of these people in your life, start praying.

If you don't have anyone earthly to talk to, talk to your Eternal Father in heaven. He is always there, eager to not only listen but eager to speak back as well.

*****

Always remember: you might feel alone, but you aren't. Easier said than done, I know, but these are the times that Jesus is bettering you for His kingdom. Trust me, it was—and still is—in my periods of loneliness where I grow the most in my faith.

Second, always remember that simply at the mention of His name, Jesus is there. No, He's not some genie in a bottle that pops up at your beck and call. He's always there. Always.

Lastly, I want to encourage you: if you're in this boat or if you have been in this boat or even if you haven't, one day, you will be. And I know, trust me, I know how hard being in this place can be. That's why prayer is so extremely crucial and vital in your walk with the Lord. Just pray. Simply talk to God. And even though it is, in fact, sometimes lonely walking in the light, never forget that you have a sovereign God who is so much bigger than your loneliness.

*****

Be strong and courageous. Do not be afraid or terrified, for the Lord your God goes with you; He will never leave you nor forsake you.
—Deuteronomy 31:6

CHAPTER 3

WALKING IN THE LIGHT

Part 2: "I'll Never Be Enough"

"I'll never be enough..."

These words, man, I can't tell you how many times the enemy has tried to convince of me this.

"Lauren, you aren't enough."

"You'll never be enough."

"You aren't worthy."

"You aren't beautiful."

These phrases, these lies—they are simply from Satan. I know you've heard these voices too.

Let me tell you something. They are from the enemy. The Bible says in John 10:10 that Satan only comes to steal, kill, and destroy.

And, my love, that's exactly what he's attempting to do with these words. He's trying to STEAL your joy, KILL your spirit, and DESTROY your faith.

You might be wondering why I'm talking about this topic underneath the chapter "Walking in the Light." I chose to write about this in this realm because when you give your life to Jesus and open up your heart to Him, you are opening up yourself to the enemy too. We are at war with the enemy every day we're on this earth. You can choose to let him win, or you can rebuke him in the name of Jesus. When you publicly proclaim and live your life boldly for Jesus against the things of this world, the devil takes that opportunity to attack you at all costs. He knows your weaknesses, and he will use them.

"How do I rebuke him? "What do I do that lets him win?"

By living in this world, giving into your fleshly desires, and living against God's word and will, you are letting the devil win. You're giving him what he wants. You can rebuke him simply by mentioning Jesus's name; the Bible also says that the enemy flees at the mention of God's name. Pray the enemy away. Pray for Jesus to protect you from the enemy's ways. Pray for courage and strength to fight back which you can do, but only with Jesus by your side. And, friend, with Jesus by your side and when you live your life completely in surrender to Jesus, that is when the enemy will try to get to you the most. How do I know this?

I know this because of my personal experience. I'm going to tell you another story.

*****

13 Reasons Why NOT

In April of 2017, I released a blog post titled "13 Reasons Why NOT." You might recognize the title as this post went viral. The hit Netflix series *13 Reasons Why* had just come out; and, yes, I did binge-watch it. After I finished the series, I decided I needed to write something in response. It's one of those things I can't really explain; it was just the Holy Spirit.

It's really a crazy story because normally I write my blogs over the course of a few days. But this one, I sat down in the middle of a Wednesday night and wrote in about twenty minutes. Y'all, it blew up. I'm normally super OCD about checking my analytics, which is basically views or hits, and I didn't check it for about twenty-four hours after I wrote it. I opened my analytics up that Friday, and it had over thirty thousand views, growing by the minute. I was freaking out. That might not sound like a lot, and in reality, it isn't. But it wasn't over. Over the course of the next few days, it grew to over seven hundred thousand page views, eventually hitting one million.

Yes, one million.

I was freaking out. I got calls from several local news channels, even a few national ones. So many eyes were on me and my heart because that's what I shared—I simply shared my heart.

LAUREN FAITH McROBERTS

In the midst of all of this, I remembered my mom asking me this, "If you could explain how you feel in one word, what would it be?"

My answer? "Vulnerable."

I was in awe, not of myself, but of Jesus.

I was completely in awe of the platform Jesus had just given me. It was one of the most exciting, spirit-filled, and essentially one of the biggest "spiritual highs" I've yet to experience in my lifetime.

But, friends, let me tell you just like I said a page back: The enemy uses these times to attack you to your core.

I had no idea what was coming. I had so many hateful e-mails, tweets, DMs, and messages. Whatever you can think of, I received it. And I'm not just talking "Oh, Lauren, I hate what you said and I don't agree with it." I'm talking "cried myself to sleep, attacking me personally, 'I'm never writing again'" thought-causing types of comments or messages. And, yes, if you noticed or wondered, that's a small part of the reason I didn't publish anything for a while after my post went viral.

Simply put, I was shaken to the core.

The enemy was trying to use so many different things to try and implant those hurtful, discouraging voices into my spirit and mind simply because I was living for Jesus. By listening and believing these voices, I was letting the enemy win.

And, unfortunately, it worked. I tried so hard to not let it get to me, but he got me right where he wanted me and used it to his advantage. Kind of sounds like a jerk thing a bad boyfriend would do, doesn't it? Put it however you want to, compare it to whatever. But it was so tough. He took so much away from me, and we cannot let him do that. This period of time in my life where I was supposed to be living life to the fullest, taking advantage of every opportunity that came my way, in love and sold out for Jesus, I let the devil win.

During the month where I was letting the enemy win in my mind and thoughts, I made a personal vow to always rebuke him and to never let him win again in my life.

So with that being said, I said previously to rebuke him, and that's what you have to do. When you're "walking in the light," you're going to be put in circumstances where you feel like you're under attack. That's when prayer and an intimate relationship with Jesus comes to be even more crucial in your life.

To end this chapter, I want to say this:

> You ARE enough.
> You ARE worthy.
> You ARE a beautiful soul.

And most importantly, you ARE a child of a God—
the ONE true God who is mighty, sovereign,
and SO MUCH BIGGER than the enemy.
Jesus has already won the ultimate
battle. He defeated death.
Who are you letting win in your personal life?

CHAPTER 3

WALKING IN THE LIGHT

Part 3: "Tempted"

What comes to mind when you hear the word "temptation"? Chocolate? Chick-Fil-A? The old-school Motown group?

Whatever it may be, I'm going to talk about a little bit deeper-type of temptation. I know, bummer, I love me some "Christian chicken" and chocolate for that matter. But this type of temptation is something, as Christ's followers, we deal with on a daily basis—the temptation to live for the world. Whether it be gossip, foul language, premarital sex, drugs, lying, or pride—whatever it is for you—we all fall short, are tempted, or give in to temptation sometimes.

Now let me clear this up. Being tempted is *not* a sin in itself. Jesus was tempted. Giving in to temptation is when we fall short of the glory of God (Romans 3:23).

The specific type of temptation I'm going to talk about for the next few pages is a broad spectrum. So I want you to think to yourself and fill in the blank with whatever personal temptation you struggle with.

*****

I struggle with a lot of different types of temptations. But for the time being, I'm going to discuss in general how I feel that, as Christians, we all struggle with at some point in our walk with the Lord—doubt.

During a specific time in high school, I would often experience periods of self-doubt and even sometimes doubt Jesus Himself.

Let me explain. Going into high school, I was completely sold out for Christ; and luckily, I never wavered. But was I tempted? Absolutely. Entering a huge school with older kids and where following Jesus wasn't necessarily the "in" thing to do, many temptations were present. Yes, there were lots of drugs, alcohol, and sex—the whole nine yards; and honestly, those things were things I never struggled with. I struggled with not fitting in with my peers and ultimately hiding my faith, not being the bold person I normally was. I don't really have a solid explanation for this except the fact that I just wanted to fit in. I wanted to keep my huge group of friends, and unfortunately, that just wasn't an option when it came to the way they were living. I couldn't stand the foul language, drugs, partying, alcohol, and gossip that they were into.

Now let me be clear. Did I write them off? Absolutely not. As a Christian, we *cannot* put ourselves in a religious bubble. Jesus fellowshipped with tax collectors and prostitutes. And frankly, He calls us to do the same. And don't get me wrong; I am in no way superior to them. We all struggle in our own ways with sin. But as I said, these friends of mine were far away from the Lord. Were they professing that they were a Christian? Yes. Were they walking the walk, not just talking the talk? Nope. I couldn't let myself fall into the temptation of changing my ways to fit in.

In Matthew 10:33, Jesus says: "If you deny Me in front of your friends, I will deny you in front of My Father in heaven."

Whoa. Let that sink in.

Can you imagine getting to heaven someday and Jesus denying you and saying He never knew you because you didn't live for Him in public?

What I mean by this is, when you're following Jesus and living for Him with all you've got, you are going to be tempted. You have a choice though. Will you give in? Or will you profess your faith in Jesus and live for Him in your actions?

Some ways you can refrain from giving in are the following:

1. Surround yourself with others that share your beliefs and are living their faith out.
2. Pray. Pray. Pray. Talk to Jesus. During these times, He is your best friend.
3. Find a mentor—someone that's older that can share in your struggles and give you advice because they've been there.
4. Dig into God's Word. Read about Thomas and how he overcame doubt, or about Job and how he kept his faith even during the worst of times.
5. Finally, whatever you put in, you will get in return. Fill your spirit with things not of this world but of Jesus. If you're struggling with negativity or foul language, don't listen to music that has these things in it. Same thing goes for what you're watching.

While it may be hard temporarily, remember that you have an eternal reward with Jesus in heaven.

*****

The right thing to do is often the hardest thing.
—My Mama

CHAPTER 4

HOUSE OF PRAYER

Out of one hundred mental health professionals, 65 percent report that a lack of communication is the number one reason for a failed relationship. You might want to ask me, "How in the world does that relate to the title 'House of Prayer'?"

Let me ask you this, what's the number one way to communicate with God?

Prayer.

What is our walk with Jesus based on?

A relationship.

See what I'm getting at?

In other words, communication seems to be key in our earthly relationships. Why should our relationship with Jesus be any different?

If you went weeks or even days without communicating with someone you had a close relationship with, I think it's fair to say the relationship would begin to suffer.

Is that not the case with Jesus as well?

*****

In the New Testament, Jesus often refers to His temple as a "house of prayer." When we read this, we often think of a building or physical meeting place. However, He also refers to our bodies being a temple. As Christians, we are His temple. We are His house of prayer. And as Christians, we should not only be in prayer individually, but we should also come to the Lord in prayer with other believers. Matthew 18:20 says, "For where two or three are gathered in My name, I am with them."

As believers, when we gather to speak to the Lord or to lift up each other in prayer, He states that He is present. He is there with us. How awesome is that! This is one of the many reasons that prayer is so crucial in our lives as Christians. When we come together in unity to pray, the gates of hell do not stand nor will they prevail.

Here are three important things to remember when it comes to prayer:

1. Prayer is so entirely crucial in our walk with the Lord.

When we give our lives to Jesus, we are committing to develop and pursue a relationship with Him just as He has with us. Relationships aren't one-sided; they are very much two-sided. With this being said, we need to be in constant, regular, authentic communication with Jesus, which brings me to my second point.

2. Pray intentionally.

When someone talks about prayer, a few things come to my mind, some of which are the prayers I grew up reciting: "God is great. God is good. Let us thank Him for our food…," or "God our Father, God our Father, we thank You, we thank You. For our many blessings, for our many blessings, A-amen. A-amen." Even as young adults, we tend to say prayers out of routine and not out of our pursuit of a relationship. We tend to pray because we feel like we *have* to, not because we *want* to. And that's a problem. Pray with intention. Just talk to Jesus. After all, He is your friend, which leads me to my third and final point.

3. There is NO RIGHT or WRONG way to pray.

    Shocker, I know. No "thees," "thous," or "haths" needed. Talk to Him like you would normally someone you had a close relationship with. No need to put on a mask or spiff up your vocabulary to talk to your heavenly Father.

And while I believe there is no right or wrong way to pray, I do believe our prayers should embody a few things:

- Reverence: Jesus, while He is your friend, He is also the Holy of Holies. We should speak to Him as such.
- Thanks or Praise: I believe we should not run to Him with our needs before we thank Him for all He has done. I encourage you to start your prayers off with thanking Him for something whether it be a huge thing He's done or simply for another day on this earth.
- Repentance: Ask for forgiveness.
- Surrender: Living for Jesus requires us to surrender daily to the things of this world. Let Him know that you've surrendered to His will and not your own.

- Deliverance: as Christians, we all struggle with sin, and we are at a constant battle with it. Ask Jesus for deliverance from whatever you may be struggling with.

*****

These things are broken down for us in the famous prayer in Matthew 6:9–13.

>Our Father who is in Heaven
>(Reverence)
>Hallowed by Your name
>(Thanks or Praise)
>Your Kingdom come. Your will be
>done, on earth as it is in heaven.
>(Surrender)
>And forgive us of our debts as we have
>also forgiven our debtors.
>(Repentance)
>And do not lead us unto temptation,
>but deliver us from evil.
>(Deliverance)

While this prayer is often overridden or forgotten about, it is like our own personal prayer guide from Jesus Himself.

So I encourage you. Be a prayer warrior. Pray with intention, and be eager and expectant of what's to come. When you change your prayer life to one of pursuit, I promise you, your whole entire life will change for the better.

CHAPTER 5

UPHILL BATTLE

When I shared part of my personal testimony with you in chapter 1, I also told you I would write more later on perhaps the biggest part of my testimony—my struggle with clinical depression and anxiety.

When people hear those words, they tend to either be scared off or choose to shut down. I'm here to ask you to let me be real, honest, and transparent with you for the next few pages and to let down all of your walls or stigma you may have against mental health.

*****

You may remember me writing of a specific night in late October of 2015. That night just happened to be the night I let my walls down and chose to quit fighting it. Fight what? At that time for about a year, I had been struggling chronically with clinical depression and anxiety.

Now before I get into the nitty-gritty, there are two types of depression: situational and clinical. Situational is being the type of depression that you struggle with because of a certain circumstance or situation in your life—for example, a divorce, loss of a loved one, abuse, and so on.

Clinical is the type that I struggle with personally, being the type where there is a chemical imbalance in the neurotransmitters in your brain. Neither clinical or situational depression is worse than the latter; it all depends on the severity of your condition.

Before you get onto me for calling depression a "condition" or for my use of the words "illness" or "chronic," let me ask you this: If you were to break your arm, would you go to the doctor and get it fixed? Yes, you would. My philosophy is that if you're struggling with your mental health, you should treat it just as you would your physical health and get help. Whether that means you need to talk to someone, seek counsel, or be put on something to counteract the imbalance in your brain. Whatever getting help means to you, just do it. After all, your body is your temple. And, yes, that does include your mind and spirit; we are called to take care of it.

*****

My struggle with depression and anxiety started when I was fourteen. Fortunately, my mom had experience with these types of issues and knew what to do. Unfortunately for some, their family members downplay the importance of mental health or believe you can just switch you struggles on and off. Now hear me out, there were many people in my life that didn't understand. One of the hardest things I've ever experienced emotionally was when a close family member of mine told me regarding my depression to "snap out of it" and that there must be something "wrong with my faith."

Y'all. I. Was. Crushed.

To hear that from anyone is hard, but from someone you love and confide in, I was taken back big time. Sadly, I would come to find out that the stigma regarding depression and anxiety and any mental health issues really was so evident in today's society especially in the church. You would not believe how many times someone would look at me funny or question my relationship with the Lord when I would discuss my struggle with anxiety and depression.

I actually remember the first counselor my mom took me too; the counselor "prescribed" me with Bible verses and told me that these should rid me of my worry and sadness. And don't get me wrong. Memorizing scripture is important, and God's word can definitely play a big role in being therapeutic; but at the time, the problem wasn't my faith. I began to dig into God's word like never before, becoming acquainted with Job and his battle with depression and Esther and her story of how Jesus used her battle for something much more.

*****

This year of my life was full of a bunch of question marks and long emotional nights. During this time when we had no answers, no doctors were taking me seriously resulting in waiting list after waiting list. It felt like the only people on my side were my parents and Jesus. Slowly but surely, I was losing contact of all friendships, relationships, and normalcy that I had always known. This sickness was affecting every single aspect of my life; I started struggling academically. I never felt good physically, I couldn't get out of the house, and frankly, I felt unheard. Every psychiatrist that my mom could get me into told me what I was dealing with was your "normal everyday anxiety" and occasional "down periods." And all counsel that I sought out told me something was wrong with my faith or looked at me like I had two heads because they simply didn't understand.

While this period in my life was filled with many unproductive nights just lying in bed with tears rolling down my face sleeping constantly because I had no energy, something else was happening to me. I was beginning to realize the weight of what I was struggling with and all of the stigmatic walls that needed to be knocked down in our society as a whole. A passion like I'd never really felt before began to take place in my spirit, and I became relentless in my pursuit of taking it upon myself to knock these walls down.

So I started writing, and not for myself, but for the whole world. I started a little blog that I called *Living Out Transparent Faith*. Every time someone at church or someone I knew would tell me something was wrong with my faith or anything along those lines, the passion inside of me kept building. And out of the blue on one school night, I decided to publish a blog post titled "My Story." Simple, I know, but it is so deep when you actually took it to heart. I'm sure people were just expecting to open it up and read surface-level facts about my life; but little did they know that everything I'd been struggling with, the reason I left public school, and why my relationships were fading were it was all within those words "I'm fighting an ongoing battle with clinical depression and anxiety."

*****

In sharing these words, I knew I was opening myself up to so many different possible outcomes. I honestly didn't know what to expect; all I knew is that the passion that Jesus had given me to share my story was undeniable, and I was determined to do all it took to obey Him and shake the stigma against mental health. That's also part of why I'm writing this for you.

My heart is so broken for those who haven't shared their stories and are still in that bondage of not living transparently. My entire life changed when I let go of my fear and simply told my story. And maybe for you, it's not a battle with your mental health. Maybe you're struggling with publicly professing your faith, lying, cheating, physical illness, divorce, purity; but whatever it is, we all have a battle. Something we've been given to conquer only through walking with Jesus. All the enemy wants for us is to lose our battle and fall into his hands and not Jesus's. It's so easy to turn from God in the midst of "our fight." It's so easy to claim the victory for the enemy and not for our mighty God or to be angry with God and give up the fight. Were there moments where I was mad at God? Were there moments were all I could do was question and doubt God? Absolutely. I was so angry with Him at moments and all I could do was wonder "why me?" or "what's your purpose for this?" It's so important to keep in mind that no matter what we face, no matter how tough our battle is, there is *always* a purpose. For me, even though my battle isn't near over, the purpose was to fight publicly and transparently so that others would know that they aren't alone. While battling with depression and anxiety would be something I'd deal with for the rest of my days, I like to say that Jesus turned my mess into a message and my tragedy into a mighty triumph. In Christ alone, I have the ultimate victory with Him.

*****

Whatever your battle is, fight it with all you've got and only in Jesus' name. I promise you: Even if your prize is in eternity and not here on this earth, He has a purpose. You will go through days where you attempt giving up or where all you can do is cry out to God in anger or doubt. During these times, draw near to Him and rally around your battle in prayer. Don't underestimate the power of His words either. In Hebrews 4:12, it says, "For the word of God is alive and active. Sharper than any double-edged sword, it penetrates even to dividing soul and spirit, joints and marrow; it judges the thoughts and attitudes of the heart."

His word is able to fight with you and *for* you. Jesus goes before you and stands with you all throughout your fight, no matter how ugly it may seem.

Remember Job and have hope like Esther. For He *is* able to turn what seems like a mess at the time into a victorious message. Never lose hope in Him. After all, He *is* on your side.

CHAPTER 6

JOY AND HAPPINESS: WHAT'S THE DIFFERENCE?

I know what you're probably thinking: There is no difference between joy and happiness.

Well, lucky for you, I'm going to argue against that point.

Joy is sustaining; happiness is fleeting.

Joy is eternal; happiness is temporary.

Joy is an attitude of the heart; happiness is merely an emotion.

See what I'm getting at?

*****

When you inherit and experience the love of Jesus, you obtain a joy that is like no other—a joy that can't described by the word "happiness."

For example, when you go through a "storm" in life, you most likely aren't happy. However, if you're going through that storm and you have an intimate relationship with Jesus, you will have joy. A common misconception about Jesus's followers is that you'll always be happy and bubbly no matter what comes your way for the rest of your life. And boy, oh boy, is that the furthest from the truth. But—and this is a *huge* but—with Jesus, you will *always* have joy.

Does this look like smiles for days and never-ending laughs? *No.* This *does* mean through your storm and through heartbreak and hard times that you will have a sustained, content, and *joyful* heart.

*****

I've grown up hearing, "Choose joy." In fact, if you were to come to my house right now, you'd probably see a big chalkboard by our kitchen with the words "Today, I will choose joy." on it. My mom never let me go through a time when I wasn't reminded of this.

One of my most favorite stories in the Bible is the one of Job. Job was a man after God's own heart that got pummeled with trials and tribulations—attacking his health, wealth, and family in a very short amount of time. Can you imagine if your valuables and the life and family you'd built was just taken right from underneath your nose? If I'm honest, I would probably be shaking a very angry fist up at God.

In Job 1:6–12 is perhaps one of the hardest conversations in the Bible to stomach and comprehend that took place. This conversation is between God and Satan. It goes as follows:

> One day the angels came to present themselves before the Lord, and Satan also came with them. The Lord said to Satan, "Where have you come from?"

> Satan answered the Lord, "From roaming throughout the earth, going back and forth on it."

> Then the Lord said to Satan, "Have you considered my servant Job? There is no one on earth like him; he is blameless and upright, a man who fears God and shuns evil."

> "Does Job fear God for nothing?" Satan replied. "Have you not put a hedge around him and his household and everything he has? You have blessed the work of his hands, so that his flocks and herds are spread throughout the land. But now stretch out

> your hand and strike everything he has, and he will surely curse you to your face."
>
> The Lord said to Satan, "Very well, then, everything he has is in your power, but on the man himself do not lay a finger."
>
> Then Satan went out from the presence of the Lord.

Basically, Satan comes to God after "roaming the earth," and God tells Satan about Job—that he is a righteous and God-fearing man that would never curse the Lord. Satan then asks to what extent has God tested Job and has he tested him regarding taking his household from him. God then replied that Satan could taunt and test Job to every extent as long as he spared Job's life. Job then undergoes countless trials and hardships, often being angry with and questioning God.

But get this: Job never doubted God's goodness. He never doubted that God had a "prosperous plan for his life, a hope and a future" for his family (Jeremiah 29:11). Instead of listening to his wife and peers who were telling him to confess his sins (basically saying his circumstances were his fault), and to curse God, Job remained faithful.

This, my friend, is *true* joy.

Job trusted God through losing his family, his belongings, his everything. He might not have been happy, but he remained joyful.

Would you—or better yet—could you do the same?

It is very important to ask ourselves these questions.

Are there things in your life you couldn't lose without cursing God?

Are there areas of your faith where you're lacking true joy?

If you answered yes to either of those questions, hear this: God *wasn't at all* surprised by your answer. Our God is an all-knowing God. And let me encourage you with this: I've been there. I have had to do some major soul-searching when it comes to the topic of joy. Joy is a hard thing to find in life, and we often search for it in all the wrong places—relationships, sex, drugs, alcohol, acceptance, friends, food, a spouse, even religion—whatever it is for you. I encourage you right now to give it to the Lord.

*****

There are three places you can be at right now—in a storm, coming out of a storm, or about to enter a storm. During any of these times when you may be losing faith, I advise you to read the story of Job. Be encouraged by His courage and faithfulness.

A relationship with God is one of complete surrender. Whatever is robbing you of your joy, give it to Jesus. In fact, when I find something is taking the place of joy in my life, this is a prayer I pray:

Dear Jesus,
Thank you for the opportunity to live in joy with you.
Thank you for that because of You, we don't have to
be on a constant search for joy. You are our joy.
I'm sorry that I've been looking in all the
wrong places when you're ever-so-persistently
knocking at the door of my heart and showing
me the joy that is a relationship with You.
Search my heart and show me the things of this earth that
are robbing me of the readily available eternal joy in You.
Help me to be in constant pursuit of the
only sustaining joy that there is.
I pray this in Your holy name. Amen.

Simple, huh? You have to mean it with all of your heart. And trust me when I say when you ask Jesus to search your heart and show you something, He *will* show you. You might not like the answer, but it *will* be revealed, I can promise you that.

And for those of you that are searching and longing to fill that hole in your heart and are tired of being happy and not joyful, I encourage you to give your life to Jesus. Commit right now to start pursuing a lifelong relationship with Him. It's never too late. I can also promise that while "walking in the light" isn't always the easiest road, you'll never regret it. Giving your life to Jesus truly is a game changer. You will never look back.

So here's to surrender, eternal joy, and *never* looking back. I'm so joyous to know I can share these little tidbits of wisdom with you. Joy changed my life; I know it can change yours as well.

LAUREN FAITH McROBERTS

CHAPTER 7

"WHERE ARE YOU?"

Alright, bear with me, I'm going to tell you yet another story. But wait, don't close your book yet; this time, it's not my story. This story comes straight out of the Bible specifically the book of Genesis. I know, I know; I'm taking it way back. But I have a really strong feeling I'm going to tell this story a wee-bit different than you might have heard it in Sunday school or Veggie Tales.

****

I'm sure you've heard of the story of the Garden of Eden, Adam, Eve, the tree, forbidden fruit, the serpent, and so on. If not, or if you need a refresher, here's the passage from Genesis 3:1–9.

> Now the serpent was more crafty than any of the wild animals the Lord God had made. He said to the woman, "Did God really say, 'You must not eat from any tree in the garden'?"

The woman said to the serpent, "We may eat fruit from the trees in the garden, but God did say, 'You must not eat fruit from the tree that is in the middle of the garden, and you must not touch it, or you will die.'"

"You will not certainly die," the serpent said to the woman. "For God knows that when you eat from it your eyes will be opened, and you will be like God, knowing good and evil."

When the woman saw that the fruit of the tree was good for food and pleasing to the eye, and also desirable for gaining wisdom, she took some and ate it. She also gave some to her husband, who was with her, and he ate it. Then the eyes of both of them were opened, and they realized they were naked; so they sewed fig leaves together and made coverings for themselves.

Then the man and his wife heard the sound of the Lord God as he was walking in the garden in the cool of the day, and they hid from the Lord God among the trees of the garden. But the Lord God called to the man, "Where are you?"

Up until this point, God had created the earth, sun, moon, stars, animals, along with Adam and Eve. At this point in time, sin had not yet entered the world; and what we like to refer to as "the fall" had not taken place, up until verse six. God had commanded Eve not to eat from one specific tree in the garden, and the devil made Eve question, "What kind of God would not let me eat from this tree He created?" Eve proceeded to eat it, therefore sinning; and that's when sin entered the world.

Now my purpose in telling you this isn't to teach you about when sin entered the world and when we were separated from God. Rather, I'm telling you this because of a verse that comes not long after the fall. Once sin entered the world, Adam and Eve realized that they were naked; and in result, they "hid" from God. In verse nine, we see where God calls out in the garden to Adam and Eve. "Where are you?"

Wait a second.

Now do you *really* believe that our all-powerful, omniscient, *all-knowing* God of the universe didn't know where they were?

Of course, He knew where they were!

He *is* omnipresent, after all, which brings me to this: If God knew where Adam and Eve were in the garden, *why* did He proceed to ask where they were?

You've probably read and heard this part of the story a million times, and that specific question has never crossed your mind. Get this; it's an extremely crucial part of the story to dissect and comprehend.

When God asked Adam and Eve "Where are you?", He wasn't asking for their physical location. He was asking where their *hearts* were.

Take a minute to think about that.

Can you imagine just having betrayed your Holy Maker and then He asks you where your heart is?

Whoa.

I also see this as God being the God of grace that He is and giving them the opportunity to fess up and have a second chance.

You see, in this specific moment along with the ones leading up to this, Adam and Eve had a choice. They could've chosen to surrender, obey, and live for God; or they could've done the latter, which they did, and betrayed God and "hid" from Him. Their hearts were not with their King; their hearts were in this world, and they had fallen short.

So with all of this being said, *you* have a choice too. You can choose to live in this world and disobey your heavenly Father. Or you can listen to the doubt and lies the enemy whispers in your ear.

Where are you? Better yet, where is your heart, dear friend?

CHAPTER 8

IN LOVE WITH LOVE (FEATURING A LETTER TO MY GIRLS)

Extraordinary florals, a bohemian aesthetic, Jesus-centered, super fun reception under strung lights, navy tuxes, old colors—all things that I picture my wedding day details to include. You're probably thinking I'm crazy. After all, I am only sixteen years old. But I feel like to some extent, everybody—or at least every girl—has thought about their wedding day.

Okay, I confess, most people probably don't know quite as many details they want as I do. If this helps at all, I *am* a hopeless romantic (ha!). God bless my future husband and my parents come my wedding day, they don't know what'll be handed to them when it comes to my perfectionistic personality. Anyways, yes, I love the thought of planning my wedding, spending the rest of my life with my "someone," and all the things that come with the future.

Now growing up, I had this plan. I was going to meet my prince charming in high school, go to prom with him, graduate with him, be high-school sweethearts, get married young, build a family together, yada yada yada.

It's really funny, because jokes on me, I'm graduating this year single as a Pringle; and I'm homeschooled—not necessarily the most ideal situation to succeed and fit into my "plan."

In this area of my life, romance, God obviously had different plans—plans that, in fact, completely wrecked the plans that I had made. My experience with relationships consists of a middle-school or early high-school relationship that lasted for a few years. It was as serious as you could be as a teenager who couldn't even drive.

Don't get me wrong. I thought I was going to marry this guy. He was my best friend. But to make things simple, our lives just didn't mesh as well as we had planned as we got older. We were both changing, finding our way, and this breakup just so happened to also be a part of my super hard, emotionally draining first year of high school. We were both so young, I mean, we still are. For goodness' sake, I'm only sixteen! But anyways, that's the extent of my relationship experience.

*****

While I don't have a ton of "being in a relationship" advice, I can give you a lot of advice on not settling and waiting. Oh, yes, the frivolous word "wait." Patience is key when it comes to relationships, my friends. I do know that much. There is a reason why it is one of the most important attributes we can carry as a person—otherwise known as the fruits of the Spirit.

One thing my GG has taught me and never let me forget is to "never settle." While she probably first told me this while we were shopping and I couldn't decide between two dresses or something, I've taken this to heart. Whether it be regarding clothes, friends, or—in this case—relationships, *never* settle.

*****

When I was in the sixth grade, my Sunday school teacher had us girls make a list of what attributes our future husband will have. I love making lists, and while this was close to six years ago, I still have this particular one. And let me tell you something. If you're in the season of singleness and waiting like I am, I want to tell you to do this: Pray for your future spouse. That may sound a little weird to you, but once you start doing it, your level of contentment in knowing that God is preparing "the one" just for you is so very special.

Another thing I'd tell someone in the season of waiting is to never even consider lowering your standards. Yes, this is along the same lines of my GG's advice to never settle, but this is just slightly different. I encourage you to make a list of what your desires for your future spouse are, even if you are in a relationship.

For example, my future husband will be

- a spiritual leader.
- He will love Jesus way more than he loves me.
- He will be compassionate and outgoing.
- He will pray with me and for me.
- and he will not be afraid of committing to purity or a lifelong covenant of love.

See? Not too bad. And, yes, it is a little bit more than "tall, dark, and handsome." I will tell you this though: If you're praying for your future spouse now, Jesus will provide. And if someone comes along that doesn't meet your foundational standards, let them go. Never settle.

The best relationship advice I've ever received was from a sermon I watched when I was a freshman in high school. The link was actually sent to me by a friend, and it literally changed my entire perspective on dating. The pastor was talking about how we all have a "lane"; you have your own lane, and everyone else has their own lane as well. Now your lane should be traveled down beside Jesus and not on your own, but he was saying to never venture outside your lane—or in other words, to go "looking" for someone to fulfill the hopeless romantic desire in your heart. The pastor was saying how you will know you've found the right person when you stay in *your* lane, following Jesus, and this person's lane intersects and combines with yours. Kind of like in harmony and in sync with each other.

I think what the pastor meant by this was that if you're fervently venturing outside your own lane, you're showing a level of not being content in where God has you. But when you're not constantly on the lookout for a girl or guy and you remain in sync with Jesus and His will for your life, you're showing an amount of faith in what God has for you in this particular season.

*****

So with all of that being said, girls and boys, prepare yourselves for who God has for you. Never settle. Don't lower your standards. And when all else fails, wait.

If you have the desire in your heart for a partner in life to love and further God's kingdom with, Jesus will provide one. Man is not meant to be alone. Never forget though that first, we are Christ's bride. Until you find that someone, you should be preparing yourself for him or her. You should also be covering your future spouse in prayer.

In the seasons of waiting, the most powerful prayer you can pray is "Thy will be done."

*****

A letter to my girls out there,

> Dear sweet one,
>
> I know it is so hard to not set your sights on the things of this world. While the world may tell you to put your worth in a boyfriend, your worth is in whose daughter you are.
>
> You, my love, are the daughter of the Almighty King. He goes before you and walks besides you.
>
> You are worthy.
> You are loved.
> You are beautiful.

You are complete with Jesus.

Wait for a man who LEADS you like Abraham led Sarah, FIGHTS for you like Jacob, CARES for you like Boaz did Ruth, and LOVES you like Christ loves His church.

You are so worth it.

xoxo
A girl who has been in your shoes,
LFM

CHAPTER 9

TRUE TO YOU

Personality begins where comparison leaves off. Be unique. Be memorable. Be confident. Be proud.

—Shannon L. Alder

To me, comparison is right up there with jealousy when it comes to toxic attitudes. Comparison is just as vicious. In the Bible in the story of the tower of Babel, we see how comparison, jealousy, and pride has been evident for thousands of years. If you aren't familiar with this story, it takes place in Genesis in the town of Babylon. These people were determined to build a tower to "set themselves apart" and "make a name for themselves."

Pride and comparison—both of which are evident in this story and oh-so evident in today's society. Whether it be in our friend groups; family; workplace; or where I struggle with it most, social media, it is undeniable. It's also something I believe is a huge issue and struggle or is that just me?

When I scroll through my Instagram feed or view my Snapchat stories, I can't help but compare many aspects in my life with the ones I'm seeing on my newsfeed. If I go on Instagram and I see where all my friends are on dates with their boyfriends or even just hanging out together without me, either I start comparing my weekend plans with theirs, or I become acquainted with the green-eyed monster—jealousy. Maybe for you, that looks like a job promotion you didn't get, your grades, or a college scholarship.

In fact, many times, I become so consumed with these struggles that I have to check myself out and log off of social media. The bottom line is pride, comparison, and jealousy all consume us at some point or another. And the point is, these deprive us of our true selves.

Let me explain. When you're constantly at war with others around you, trying to compete or compare your life, your body, your relationship—whatever it may be—you become trapped. These emotions are so entangling that when we suffer from them, they become a part of our identity. They start to become evident in the way we relate and talk to others, the way we treat our loved ones, how we feel about ourselves, and most importantly, affect and put a strain on our relationship with Jesus.

Jealousy will starve your joy.

Comparison will get in the way of your walk with Christ.

Pride will rob us of our true personalities.

*****

In order to keep this from happening, we have to constantly be aware of what we're feeding into our bodies whether it be on social media or what music you're listening to. Everything we consume affects the way we deal with these feelings.

And you know what it all comes down to?

Humility.

When we see something that causes us to compare ourselves or something that sparks jealousy, we have to humble ourselves and let go of our pride. If we can't do that, like I said, our true demeanor and personality will be compromised.

*****

Another thing that comes with this struggle is the struggle of boldness and confidence. With the attitude of comparison often comes cockiness. The opposite of cockiness is humility. And get this, you can still be humble and confident.

"Confidence is knowing you can get to the top. Cockiness is thinking you're already there." (Anonymous)

God calls us to be confident. He calls us to be bold and know our worth. If He didn't want us to know our worth, He wouldn't have devoted a whole chapter in the book of Psalms speaking to our intricate being and how we're "fearfully and wonderfully" made. However, with knowing our self-worth comes the responsibility of humility.

There's a fine line between confidence and humility, and cockiness and pride. It's important that we can find that line and what that looks like in our life. Surround yourself with others that encourage your contentment and don't urge you to covet. Unfortunately, we live in a society where "one-upping" is the norm. And all we can be responsible for is ourselves. When you're tempted to compare, encourage instead.

*****

We have to be willing to stop trying to make a name for ourselves, but rather, start making a name for the One who gave us one in the first place.

*****

Never be afraid to be you, and don't let pride and comparison rob you of who you truly are. God made you just the way you are, for a very specific reason and purpose.

*****

I praise You because I am fearfully and wonderfully made; Your works are wonderful, I know that full well.

Psalms 139:14

CHAPTER 11

"TETELESTAI"

"*Tetelestai*" is the Greek word for 'it is finished.' Ah, perhaps three of my favorite words ever spoken. You can find these words in the Bible in John 19:30. Jesus said these words after He, completely blameless, was arrested by the Romans and hung on the cross. These three words are quite honestly the greatest sound of triumph ever heard by this earth.

When Jesus said this, He was declaring that the battle was won, we were atoned for, and the devil had no place. All He had promised was fulfilled, and after He declared this statement, "He bowed His head and gave up His spirit" (found in John 19:28–30). Some may have thought that Jesus's death on the cross was the end, but the righteous knew that this was just the beginning. Mankind was finally atoned for because of His death, and more importantly, His resurrection three days later. We are able to live in eternity with Christ Jesus, our Lord.

The day that the world became dark for three hours was the day that the Lord our God sacrificed Himself to be crucified for *our* darkness. Two thousand years ago, someone died for *us*—someone who had never sinned and who was seemingly perfect. But He loves us *so much* that He was beaten, stoned, whipped, and nailed to a cross where His vital organs hung and His heart literally broken in half. He suffered, and He put on a crown of thorns for us.

He died a brutal death *for us*.

*****

At that moment up on that cross when He was overcome with all of the world's sins and darkness, He said to His Father:

"It is finished."

"Tetelestai." (in Hebrew)

*****

Several days before, He claimed that He was coming back. He was put in a tomb with guards surrounding it so no one would take His body. And on the third day after His death, the tomb was empty. He rose. He resurrected from the dead, just as He said He would.

*****

One of my favorite pastors said this, "The stone wasn't rolled away to let Jesus out. It was rolled away to let us in."

He was born.

He lived a life of service.

He suffered.

He died.

He rose.

And y'all, He's coming again!

Because of this day in history, when our sinless Savior was hung on the cross and died for us, *we can live forever in heaven with our Savior and Lord.*

But first, we have to let Him in.

"Here I am! I stand at the door of your heart and knock." (Revelation 3:20)

Remember, the tomb was opened not to let Jesus out but to let *us in*! And remember, when you're worried about the future or you're in a storm, we were atoned for two thousand years ago. Our lives are secured when we let Christ in and live for Him.

Death has been defeated. Satan, conquered.

It. Is. Finished.

*****

I don't quite know what my future holds, but I know for sure that I have a Father in heaven who is all-knowing and completely present. All you have to do is let Him in. Surrender your life. Everything else is finished.

Join me, and just let Jesus in.

ACKNOWLEDGMENTS

Mama, for being my rock during the darkest of times, for never giving up on me, and for believing in me.

Daddy, for always praying over me and encouraging me to continue being bold. This book is a true testament of how you've always taught me to chase after something until you achieve it.

GG, for teaching me about strength and to never settle, and for every other bit of advice you've given me.

Grandma Linda, for always speaking truth over me and reminding me that nothing is too "crazy" for Jesus to do.

Kelly, Makenna, and Isaac, for always keeping me a kid at heart and inspiring me to have a childlike faith. I love you guys with all of my heart. I pray that when you get older and go through these issues, you know you can confide in your big sissy. I hope that I've taught you that Jesus is your only constant.

Miss Hamilton, for teaching me that walking in the light is hard but so worth it.

Mama H, for being a living example that living fearlessly is oh-so worth it in the long run.

To my blog supporters, without you, I don't know if I would have realized that my story is one that needs to be told. Y'all are *so* loved.

To all of my friends and family, thank you for supporting me in all of my ambitious endeavors. Y'all have made me who I am.

Most of all, my Heavenly Father; without Jesus, these pages would've been full of empty words.

For Him and only Him,
Lauren Faith

ABOUT THE AUTHOR

Lauren is a seventeen-year-old student in South Carolina. She blogs, leads worship, speaks, and takes care of her own personal photography business in her free time. Her heart is with people and sharing how Jesus has changed her life with everyone she meets. With her passion for the Gospel comes her passion for transparency and sharing in her trials and her triumphs.

During her freshman year of high school, she was handed a crazy set of cards when she was diagnosed with severe clinical depression, anxiety, and polycystic ovarian syndrome all within a few months. Since then, she has shared in her struggles and been completely raw with everyone, seeing as that December, she started a blog. That first blog of hers just so happened to be named *Living Out Transparent Faith*. Since December of 2015, she has impacted hundreds of thousands of people through her writing and speaking opportunities, just by sharing her story.

Her hope in you reading this is that with an open heart, you would let the words God has given her bless, impact, or even change your life in some way.

CPSIA information can be obtained
at www.ICGtesting.com
Printed in the USA
LVHW072256081218
599748LV00054B/2850/P